Civil Liberties and the Miners' Dispute

First Report of the Independent Inquiry

GW00569179

National Council for Civil Liberties
1984

National Council for Civil Liberties
21 Tabard Street, London SE1 4LA

© NCCL Inquiry Panel 1984

British Library Cataloguing in Publication Data

National Council for Civil Liberties
  Civil Liberties and the Miners' Dispute:
  First Report of the Independent Inquiry
  1. Strikes and lock-outs – Miners – Great Britain – History –
  20th Century
  2. Police – Great Britain – History – 20th Century
  I. Title
  331.89'2822334'0941   HD5365.M6

  ISBN 0-946088-11-X

Phototypeset, printed and bound by Yale Press, London

PREFACE

The National Council for Civil Liberties resolved at its 1984 Annual General Meeting that an Independent Inquiry should be set up to investigate the civil liberties implications of the policing of the miners' strike. The Inquiry was established in August 1984 with the following terms of reference:

"To inquire into and thereby establish the fullest possible account and the civil liberties implications of the role of the police, the police authorities and the criminal courts in the events arising from and relating to the NUM dispute, which began in March 1984."

The members of the inquiry are:

PROFESSOR PETER WALLINGTON (Professor of Law, University of Lancaster) (Chairman)

MR JOHN ALDERSON (former Chief Constable of Devon and Cornwall)

MR LARRY GOSTIN (General Secretary, NCCL)

MRS SARAH McCABE (formerly of the Oxford University Centre for Criminological Research)

MR IAN MARTIN (General Secretary, Fabian Society)

DR CHRISTOPHER MASON (Lecturer in International Relations, University of Glasgow, and member of Strathclyde Regional Council Police and Fire Committee)

This is an Interim Report. The timing of our Final Report will depend on when the strike comes to an end. We have already received considerable help, including financial assistance, research and administrative support and evidence. Full details of the evidence and other assistance we have received will be given in our final report. For the moment we wish to express our thanks collectively to all who have assisted the inquiry in any way thus far. Since the outset of the dispute NCCL has had volunteer researchers and observers in the major mining areas, and their reports will be available to us for the preparation of our final report; but we have not been able to take full account of the results of their observations at this stage. We have also not yet had an opportunity to place the evidence in the context of the chronology of the dispute in the various areas affected; we intend to pursue this point in our Final Report.

This Report is intended first to provide a general, and generally acceptable, framework of basic civil liberties, as a perspective from which issues of civil liberties raised by the strike can be discussed; then to identify the major civil liberties issues of the strike; and finally to encourage wide discussion of the civil liberties implications of the strike before the drift towards acceptance of the denial of liberties becomes irreversible, and new policies with lower standards for the protection of freedom become acceptable by attrition.

Our Interim Report is also intended to serve one other purpose: to give us the opportunity to appeal again to all those who can do so to send us written evidence of what has happened and the civil liberties implications of the policing of the strike. We need to receive evidence, and views, from all involved, if we are to be truly comprehensive in our account of the dispute and identification of the issues. Any evidence should be sent to us as soon as possible, at 21 Tabard Street, London SE1 4LA.

1. INTRODUCTION – THE NEED FOR AN INQUIRY

1.1 By the time this report is published in December 1984, the miners' strike – if it is still in progress – will have lasted for nine months. The strike, undeniably the most serious industrial dispute since the 1920s, has been the occasion of the most massive and sustained deployment of the police ever experienced in Britain. By 8th November 1984, 7,658 arrests had been made in England and Wales alone, and large numbers of police officers and pickets had been injured; two pickets had died. Nobody can be in any doubt about the gravity of the situation.

1.2 It is against this background that we have produced an Interim Report. We cannot anticipate, writing in late November, whether the strike will have come to an end before our report is published or not. Whatever happens we believe that we must speak out in defence of those basic liberties which we fear are in danger of being overwhelmed by the magnitude of the conflict and the nature of the policing measures being adopted.

1.3 At the end of the strike we are convinced that there will be a need for an inquest on the policing of the dispute, from which proposals for legal and organisational reforms should emerge. The necessity for public debate on these will be so important that we are all firmly convinced that a formal parliamentary or judicial inquiry will be essential. In the face of the Government's manifest unwillingness to countenance such a course we offer this report as a preliminary contribution.

1.4 It is important to be clear why a civil liberties inquiry of this kind should focus primarily on the policing of the dispute. We are perfectly well aware of the violence that has occurred during this dispute and that our terms of reference have been criticised for not explicitly including this subject. As we make clear in the next section, protection from violence and fear of violence is a fundamental civil liberties principle which has been extensively violated during this dispute.

1.5 However if private individuals or organisations infringe the rights of other individuals or organisations, that is a matter for adjudication by the courts. If private individuals or organisations break the criminal law, it is the responsibility of the normal agencies of law enforcement to take action. In neither case is it a matter for an independent inquiry. But the actions of the police, and the machinery of criminal justice generally, are a different matter. They are public agencies, acting on behalf of society. The actions of the police are more than just acts of individuals; they are invested with the authority of the community on whose behalf they work.

1.6 The accountability of those who exercise this kind of power and authority – be they police or cabinet ministers – to public representatives is a pre-condition of liberty and democracy. No society can be democratic if the police are a state within a state. Accountability (which is not necessarily control) is essential to ensure that power is used for the purposes of those in whose name it is exercised, not those who exercise it; this is true of all agencies of government, but especially of those with coercive powers, such as the police.

1.7 The police role is not precisely or exhaustively defined by the law: methods of policing and the distribution of resources are greatly affected by the exercise of discretion. These are factors which determine the kind of policing we have. Moreover, because the police in Britain are not under direct political control, it is normally the police themselves and not their political masters who must be accountable for the way they discharge their duties. Regrettably, some police officers are apt to characterise public discussion of policing policy as "undermining the police". For the reasons we have given we cannot accept this attitude; on the contrary, public discussion of the role of the police may help to protect them from political manipulation. By the same token, we, and the community at large, must not attribute blame to the police for actions which *are* the result of political direction.

1.8 Police powers in the street and places of public resort are, in practice, considerable, since police officers themselves effectively make the definitions of offensive behaviour under the Public Order Act 1936 and of obstruction under the Police Act 1964 through their decisions whether to make an arrest. But most citizens are content to delegate to their local police force the task of preventing violence and maintaining free passage. The majority view is probably that, with some exceptions, the job is well done. These exceptions may be due to insensitive or downright mistaken operational decisions at a senior planning level, to insufficient or inappropriate training, or to supervision on the ground which was inadequate to control the actions of individual or groups of police officers, who abuse the power and discretion with which the community has entrusted them.

1.9 It is important to distinguish between two of these possibilities of bad policing. Operational decisions are subject to little restraint. On the other hand the actions of individual police officers on the ground can be made subject to an official complaint or even legal action, if the officer can be identified.

1.10 It would be wrong for us to attempt to investigate in detail all allegations of individual improprieties, however much the present statutory system for investigating complaints may be judged to be inadequate. One of our central tasks, however, is to consider closely the implications of the styles of policing that have been adopted during the dispute and the question of accountability for the discretionary policy decisions that determine the differing styles of policing. To both these points we also return later in this report.

1.11 In this and in our Final Report, our objective will be to be fair to the police, as individuals and as a group, and to recognise fully the context within which they have been working during the dispute. But policing policy and the actions of individual police officers must be subject to critical examination, and the police's position as the central public agency for the enforcement of law and order makes them the inevitable focus of our primary concerns. Moreover, the concerns we wish to express about the civil liberties implications of the dispute will be shared by many police officers, and by those concerned with the effectiveness and integrity of the British police – attributes which we freely acknowledge. It is no service to the preservation of these attributes to gloss over the effects of the great strains on policing and police-community relationships imposed by the dispute.

1.12 In this connection, there is clear evidence of the growth of alienation in mining communities towards the police which could affect police-community relationships on a scale not seen for many years. The principal reason for this alienation, we believe, is the belief, strongly felt by striking miners and their families, that among the purposes for which the police and the criminal justice system have been used (whether by design or not) has been the promotion of the interests of the National Coal Board and the Government. The NCB have chosen not to use the available remedies of the civil law, and the effect of some policing operations has been to prevent even peaceful picketing. In other words, many striking miners believe that the police and the courts have been used to break the strike. This perception has been aggravated by statements of politicians and others portraying the strike as a confrontation in which striking miners are a force to be "defeated"; by the highly unusual use of bail conditions to restrict the picketing activities of those charged with relatively minor offences; and above all by the disproportionate use of police resources compared to the seriousness of the threats to public order and individual rights posed by the picketing.

1.13 We believe that our recognition of the exceptional nature of the police role in this dispute, and of its implications, is also shared by senior police officers. The point was well made by a serving police inspector in a letter to *The Guardian* on 6th June, from which we quote:

> "During the miners' dispute the Government. . . has decided to use the 'thin blue line' as its battering ram against Arthur Scargill in an attempt to deliver the *'coup de grâce'* to the trade union movement as a whole. The result is that whilst trying to maintain public order in the coalfields, the police service has unwittingly allowed itself to be portrayed as Margaret Thatcher's puppet. . . . Police officers are intent on resisting interference from Government. Most importantly, I believe many officers are increasingly disturbed at the lack of care, compromise and liberty in our society. . . . In the meantime the police service has been caught in the middle, used to pursue a political goal rather than one of public duty."

This is not a solitary voice from the police. The same point was reinforced by Mr Tony Judge, official spokesman for the Police Federation of England and Wales, in a statement made in a radio broadcast at the end of October:

> "It's not simply a case of the employer saying 'well I won't go to court because it might make things worse'. Surely at the back of Mr MacGregor's mind is the knowledge that these policemen are there, that the pits of Nottinghamshire have been kept open and that people have been able to go to work almost solely because of the presence of that police force. And so it looks to us as if there has been a deliberate decision to use the police as the way of keeping the coal industry producing some coal."

The fact that such views are held in responsible police quarters makes an unanswerable case for an inquiry into the manner of policing of the dispute and the implications of that policing for civil liberties.

2. INDIVIDUAL CIVIL LIBERTIES

2.1 Civil liberties mean different things to different people. Before we can usefully explain the issues which are relevant to this Inquiry we must first explain what we understand to be those essential liberties, without which Britain would not be a free country, for which we believe there would be general support.

2.2 The freedoms we identify as fundamental, and relevant to this Inquiry, are these:

(1) Freedom of the person from physical assault or the fear of physical assault.

(2) Freedom of thought, conscience and belief.

(3) Freedom of speech and publication.

(4) Freedom to assemble peacefully for the purpose of protest or demonstration, including peaceful picketing.

(5) Freedom to travel unhindered anywhere within the country for any lawful purpose.

(6) Freedom from arbitrary or unnecessary arrest and detention.

(7) The right to be treated fairly and equally in the courts, including the presumption of innocence in criminal trials and the right to legal representation.

(8) Freedom of association for any lawful purpose, including freedom to participate in political and trade union activity.

(9) The right to withdraw one's labour.

(10) Freedom to own, enjoy and dispose of personal possessions and private property.

2.3 These freedoms are, in various ways, recognised and embodied in the general principles of both English and Scots law, and form part of the European Convention on Human Rights, which has been accepted by successive British Governments as a set of binding international obligations. A measure of the breadth of support they command is the backing given to the NCCL's Charter of Civil Rights and Liberties, to which we all subscribe, and which on its first publication in February this year was signed by some

1500 people representing a wide range of public opinion and including MPs of all the major political parties. (The Charter is reprinted as an Appendix to this Report).

2.4 Some additional comment is required on the relevance of the liberties we assert to what has happened during the coal dispute.

2.5 The first comment concerns the right to withdraw one's labour. It is a fundamental yardstick of freedom that workers may choose to participate in peaceful collective action, including the withdrawal of labour, to protect their interests. To uphold this right does not imply any particular view of the merits of the miners' strike any more than to support freedom of speech implies support for the things said by a particular speaker. It is not necessary, as well as being outside our terms of reference, for us to express a collective view on the matters in dispute between the striking miners and the NCB, or between the working miners and the NUM.

2.6 We accept that freedom not to take part in a strike is as much a fundamental right as the right to strike. Going to work during a strike is in any case a lawful activity, and like any other lawful activity ought not to be impeded by violence, threats or physical obstruction. We have identified the freedom to travel unhindered for any lawful purpose as a fundamental liberty; this is equally so whether the purpose is peaceful picketing, taking part in a demonstration, or simply going to work.

2.7 Our terms of reference do not extend to the conduct of the striking or working miners as such. Allegations of police violence do fall within our terms of reference, and we discuss them below. However, in addressing this issue we cannot ignore the reality of the strike. The police do not act in a vacuum, and any sensible examination of the policing of the strike must take fully into account the circumstances which have shaped the context of police actions and their objectives. We regard it as axiomatic that violence of any kind is inimical to the most basic liberties of its victims, as is intimidation by threats of violence. It should have had no place in this dispute. This applies not only to violence on the picket lines, whether by police or by pickets, but to violence within the mining communities against both working and striking miners or their families.

2.8 Most industrial disputes are conducted peacefully, most trade unionists reject violence in support of their objectives, and most of the participants in the present dispute have abstained from violence or threats of violence. But it is clear from the evidence we have received, as well as newspaper and television reports, that violence and threats against working miners and their families, and

6

such intimidatory actions as aggressive picketing of homes and attacks on their property, have occurred and continue to occur. Violence and threats by working miners against striking miners have so far as we can judge been less common, but clear examples have been drawn to our attention. Discussion of the civil liberties implications of the dispute requires recognition not only of the fact of violence but also of the powerful fears of loss of employment and community, and other evident stresses, that have driven many previously peaceable and law abiding citizens in this direction.

2.9 We urge all those in a position to use or threaten violence to refrain from doing so, and on those in a position of influence over others to use it to ensure that all picketing and all policing are conducted without either resort to or provocation of violence.

2.10 Over and above the question of violence by police officers, to which we return below, other police behaviour during the strike has provoked fear and hostile behaviour among pickets. The banging of police shields, apparently arbitrary arrests, the rough handling of pickets, or the waving of pay packets at pickets – all of which appear to have occurred on a number of occasions – are provocative. The police should exercise the utmost care to avoid behaving in ways which may encourage violence.

2.11 Protecting and upholding the liberties we have set out is part and parcel of the work of the police, the Police Authorities and the courts. We reject the notion that the police and supporters of civil liberties must inevitably be opponents. Our perspective is one in which we value the police as an agency which should share the same goals as civil libertarians – the protection of the rights of individuals within the law and the preservation of what Lord Scarman called "public tranquillity".

2.12 However the protection of one person's liberties can too easily be secured at the expense of those enjoyed by someone else. It is important that the police should not use methods of law enforcement which *unnecessarily* curtail the liberties of individuals affected by their actions, however important the protection of the goals. It is in this extremely difficult balancing process that there can be legitimate differences of opinion and judgment, despite agreement about objectives. The professional judgments of the police deserve respect, but whether or not the balance itself has been held must, in a democracy, be a matter for the public's judgement.

3. CIVIL LIBERTIES ISSUES RAISED BY THE DISPUTE

3.1 The civil liberties issues raised by the conduct and policing of the dispute can be divided into four broad areas: police activities in the mining communities and those other areas where picketing has taken place; the impact of the dispute outside the areas immediately affected; issues relating to the enforcement of the criminal law; and issues relating to the organisation, finance and accountability of the police. Within each of these broad headings we need to identify several specific points.

3.2 We do not attempt at this stage to reach firm conclusions, still less to make recommendations for the aftermath of the strike. We have not yet received, or had an opportunity to evaluate, much of the relevant evidence; and events continue to unfold in a climate increasingly hostile to civil liberties. We can, however, highlight the issues from some of the extensive published information, and use this, the evidence we have received and our own knowledge and observations of the dispute, to draw some provisional conclusions. We also wish, in the face of critical and increasing damage to civil liberties, to make a small number of specific and urgent recommendations. These set out actions which we believe would help to halt the erosion of liberty in the conduct of the dispute.

Issues in the mining communities and on the picket lines

Restrictions on peaceful picketing

3.3 Contrary to the impression inevitably created by media concentration on incidents of mass picketing and violent confrontation, *most* of the picketing during the strike has been orderly and on a modest scale. The organisers of the strike have arranged rotas of strikers to mount a continuous official picket at the entrance to their own pit. These official picket lines, usually limited to no more than six men at a time, have been present throughout the strike at the majority of pits. Such picketing is generally within the law. Section 15 of the Trade Union and Labour Relations Act 1974 expressly legalises peaceful picketing of a workplace in furtherance of a trade dispute for the purpose of peaceful persuasion. An important amendment to section 15, effected by the 1980 Employment Act, restricts legal picketing to the pickets' own place of work, and picketing elsewhere, generally referred to as "secondary picketing", no longer enjoys protection against civil actions – likewise attendance at a picket line by supporters not personally involved in the dispute.

3.4 In addition to the "statutory" pickets referred to above, there has been considerable secondary picketing in this dispute, both at pitheads and at a variety of other locations. However secondary picketing is not as such a criminal offence. While it is almost always likely to involve a breach of the civil law (and has in this dispute been the subject of at least one injunction), it is important to appreciate the role of the police in this context. The present Government's own Code of Practice on Picketing, issued in 1980, puts the matter clearly:

> "The police have *no* responsibility for enforcing the *civil* law. An employer cannot require the police to help in identifying the picket against whom he wishes to seek an order from the civil court. Nor is it the job of the police to enforce the terms of an order." (Paragraph 27; italics in original).

3.5 The fact that picketing does not constitute a criminal offence does not of course end the matter, because the police have a further duty to preserve the peace, which may involve restraining the actions of even an orderly picket line if this is necessary in order to prevent anticipated disorder. Generally the police discharge this difficult responsibility sensibly and sensitively, and they have frequently done so during the miners' strike.

3.6 We have, however, been concerned to receive evidence of apparently unnecessary cordoning off of small groups of pickets while buses containing working miners, or convoys of coal lorries, pass at speed. Such actions are at variance with the common, and sensible, practice of the police in previous industrial disputes of stopping vehicles on behalf of the pickets to give the latter a reasonable opportunity to speak to the drivers. (Pickets themselves cannot legally compel drivers to stop.)

3.7 We believe the cordoning off of pickets should be avoided whenever possible, since it can easily create the impression of partisanship. In particular there is no justification for cordoning off pickets simply because they are engaged in secondary picketing in breach of the civil law. To do so is contrary to the Code of Practice, as well as involving the taking of sides in the dispute. We shall return to this issue in our final report, and would welcome evidence on the policing of small and orderly picket lines as well as the policing of mass picketing.

Mass pickets

3.8 Although less frequently than picketing in small numbers, mass picketing has occurred on a large number of occasions, and a significant minority of the mass pickets have involved violent clashes between pickets and police. Much of the violence, many of the injuries and many of the arrests in this dispute have occurred during mass picketing. Some of the most horrifying incidents of violence, vividly portrayed in the media, took place on such occasions. Like very many other people, we have been shocked both by the sight of pickets throwing missiles and of vehicles overturned and set alight, and by the sight of police officers on horseback charging into crowds and wielding batons.

3.9 There have been demands for legislation to ban mass picketing. We would however be opposed to any such measures.

3.10 Not all mass picketing is intended to be intimidatory or to prevent free passage. Strikers and their supporters, like every other citizen, have the right to assemble peacefully for the purpose of demonstration or protest, and that right must be defended whether or not the venue for the demonstration happens to be the colliery gates. Indeed the police normally do treat mass pickets as "demonstrations".

3.11 Moreover in practical terms a ban on mass picketing would be extremely difficult to enforce without the risk of increasing any disorder, and its non-enforcement, however justifiable, would tend to bring the law into disrepute. It is better that the police should rely on existing provisions of the criminal law such as behaviour likely to lead to a breach of the peace, or obstruction of the highway.

3.12 We cannot in any event divorce the phenomenon of protest from its causes. The presence of the police in large numbers, to secure the entry of miners or the exit of coal, and the presence and behaviour of the pickets are as inextricably interrelated as the proverbial chicken and egg. It is an oversimplification merely to say that the police would not be there but for the pickets.

Police policy towards mass picketing

3.13 The policy of the police towards mass picketing raises critical issues. It is perhaps one of the most intractable problems of policing.

3.14 In discussing these issues we start from the proposition that any person has the right to choose whether or not to go to his or her work place so long as it is not for an unlawful purpose. The police have a responsibility to protect the right of individuals to go to work free from harm or threats to themselves or their families, even if their action is repugnant to their fellows. Police activity to prevent and deal with violence or threatened violence is correct and indeed essential. So too must the police be seen to understand and to enforce the essential right to picket peacefully.

3.15 Thus the police have a duty to protect the civil liberties of all sides in an industrial dispute. But in enforcing those rights they have a choice. They can enforce the right come what may by using whatever force is necessary. Alternatively they can exercise their discretion not to enforce a right in a particular case because in their view it would lead to more, not less, disorder or violence. Similarly, the police may decide not to act in a particular case because to do so would commit resources which are more urgently needed for their work elsewhere. Effective policing should not be measured solely by the ability to enforce the law on every occasion. The public should not expect, for example, that *any* amount of force would be justified to ensure that a person could go to the work place, especially at the risk of provoking serious disorder or danger to the safety of others.

3.16 There have been a number of instances of the use of disproportionate police resources to accompany individuals to work. A recent example was at Cortonwood colliery on 9th November, where the first striker who had returned to work was accompanied by between 1,000 and 2,000 police officers. In addition to being an inappropriate use of scarce police resources, such decisions promote disharmony and discontent among those picketing; this can contribute to alienation and ultimately more public disorder.

3.17 We understand the symbolic value of enforcing the right of those who wish to cross picket lines to be able to do so. The symbols are twofold – one appropriate, and one not so. The first is the symbol of enforcement of the law of the land: we recognise this as a compelling argument, though not always conclusive. The second is the symbol often perceived by striking miners – "breaking the strike", or publicly encouraging other miners to cross picket lines.

3.18 We accept therefore that it is a legitimate use of police resources to ensure that working miners can travel to work – but not at *any* cost. The police decision is an operational one which must be affected by, among other things, the number of people who wish to travel to work, the number of pickets and whether there is a probability that enforcement of the law will cause public disorder. It is a matter of serious concern that decisions of this nature should be the subject of proper accountability, a point to which we return.

3.19 Once the police have made the operational decision whether to enforce the law in a particular situation, they should pursue that course of action with the minimum use of confrontation; they should impose as few restrictions and as little compulsion as possible; and they should behave in such a way as to cause the least possible violence. That police behaviour in controlling any demonstration, including mass pickets, should be free from aggression or violence is made clear in the present Government's Green Paper on public order published in 1980. Discussing the control of crowds or demonstrations, the Government spelt out its commitment to policing by consent:

"The British police do not have sophisticated riot equipment – such as tear gas or water cannon – to handle demonstrations. Their traditional approach is to deploy large numbers of officers in ordinary uniform in the passive containment of a crowd. Neither the Government nor the police wish to see this approach abandoned in favour of more aggressive methods." *(Review of the Public Order Act 1936 and related legislation,* Cmnd. 7891, para.15).

3.20 Matters have changed very considerably since this was written four years ago. The substantial extension of riot training following the inner city riots of 1981, and the Home Office's requirement for all police forces to set up Police Support Units, have led to a different approach to the policing of large-scale demonstrations. The first real test of the new training and organisation has been in this dispute, and it has been evident that a much more assertive approach has been adopted by many police officers than would have been expected in the past.

3.21 In the earlier stages of the dispute, the traditional approach was followed. On many occasions large numbers of police have confronted equally large numbers of pickets with little more than pushing and shoving as a consequence. However it is perfectly clear to us, from first hand evidence we have received and from numerous press, radio and television reports, that a policy of passive containment has not been applied universally or consistently. Demonstrations have been broken up by police on horseback and with dogs, and police vans with protective wings and shields have been used to drive back crowds or force a passage for vehicles. There is also evidence of inconsistency and unpredictability in the response of the police to particular actions of pickets on different occasions.

3.22 We accept, of course, the necessity for firm action to prevent and quell serious disorder. We accept the need for proper protective equipment, including riot shields for police on duty under a bombardment of missiles. There are however several matters of serious concern in the way in which the police have responded to mass picketing:

(i) *Violence*. As we have made clear we condemn all violence; but we are inevitably particularly concerned over police officers using violence, since this is the antithesis of the duties they are paid to perform. The use of force in self-defence, to protect others or to enforce the law may be unavoidable. Where avoidable violence is alleged, we would expect the fullest investigation. We have been particularly concerned by a pattern of complaints relating to three matters: assaults on pickets during picketing, on occasion resulting in serious injuries to the pickets; individuals travelling to or from picket lines being assaulted, without apparent provocation, by police officers; and deliberate damaging of the property, particularly the cars, of pickets travelling to or from picket lines. We should welcome further evidence, in particular of the outcome of investigations where such complaints have been followed up.

(ii) *Provocative, insensitive and unprofessional actions by police officers*. Police officers are human and like anyone else can behave tactlessly or overreact on occasion. The tasks of police trainers and supervising officers on the spot is to minimise the occurrence of these human failings. This is especially important as the divisions caused by the dispute deepen, and those whom the police confront become increasingly frustrated and embittered. We are disturbed by widespread complaints, often corroborated by news reports, of such behaviour as rhythmic drumming of batons on riot shields, personal remarks and insults directed at striking miners and their wives, the waving of pay packets and lines of police applauding as injured pickets are carried away. It appears to us that the new philosophy of training, and particularly the training and organisation of the Police Support Units, may not only have been inadequate to prevent these actions but, by emphasising the group ethic, may have encouraged them.

(iii) *Over-readiness to break up crowds*. The frequency with which the policy of passive containment has been departed from in favour of dispersal concerns us. We are not in a position at this stage to judge whether dispersal tactics have always been operationally essential; we would welcome more evidence, from police and pickets as well as independent eye-witnesses, on this point. It is a matter for speculation whether there would have been less stone-throwing or violence if mounted police had not been used.

(iv) *The use of snatch squads.* The technique of the "snatch squad" is a relatively recent development in policing. A close formation of police officers in the shape of a wedge is used to break up a crowd. The wedge is followed by other officers who make "snatch" arrests from among the crowd. The "snatch squad" should only be used to arrest a particular individual identified as a ringleader or having thrown a missile, but it is all too easy for a genuine mistake to be made, and the wrong person to be arrested. It has been alleged that on many occasions arrests have been purely random and not directed at ringleaders. Even if this is not so, it must often have appeared to those in the crowd to be so. The attempt may lead to resistance, assaults, even injuries, and is likely to exacerbate the risk of serious disorder and be greatly resented by the colleagues of the arrested man. It appears to us that those directing police operations on the spot have underestimated these factors, and used snatch squads more frequently than circumstances warranted. We consider this practice should be urgently reviewed.

(v) *Over-reaction to slogans.* It is only to be expected that pickets will pass uncomplimentary remarks at those crossing the picket line to go to work. We accept that freedom of speech does not extend to issuing threats of violence or using words calculated to put others in fear. We suspect, however, that most people would be surprised that a picket shouting "scab" at those crossing the picket line should be arrested for a criminal offence. It must be a very rare case that someone is intimidated merely by the addition of slogans to the presence of a line of pickets, and the substantial presence of the police will ensure that the shouting of itself does not lead to a breach of the peace. We have therefore been disturbed to receive reports of pickets in some areas being arrested or threatened with arrest for shouting "scab" or similar epithets. We question the wisdom of such arrests, which we believe to be unnecessary, unduly restrictive of freedom of speech and more likely to provoke than to prevent breaches of the peace.

The police in the mining communities

3.23 The reason generally given for the presence of the police in very large numbers on the streets of many mining communities is intimidation or fears of intimidation of working miners and their families. There have been instances, particularly in the earlier stages of the strike in those areas where the strike was not solidly supported, of the picketing of the homes of working miners, usually at times when they were seeking to go to, or return from, work. Sometimes considerable numbers of pickets have gathered. While usually there has been no evidence of any intention to be violent (notable exceptions have occurred such as the throwing of bricks through windows), the effect of the picketing has been to engender fear in the families concerned, many of whom have been afraid to leave their homes during the picketing. Other incidents of intimidation, some extremely serious, including attacks on individuals and on houses and cars, and threats made to wives and children, have been very fully documented in the national press. Intimidation of or attacks on striking miners and their families have also been drawn to our attention, but have received less publicity and, so far as we can judge, less response from the police.

3.24 We have no reason to believe that intimidatory tactics have been resorted to by more than a small minority of either striking or working miners. We condemn the use or threat of violence or other criminal acts adopted to "persuade" individuals not to work – or not to strike. We accept that the incidence of intimidation requires a police response. The ways in which some police have carried out their duties to protect individuals have however given rise to some specific concerns:

(i) *Undue restrictions on freedom of movement.* We develop this point, which is not limited to the mining communities, later.

(ii) *Arbitrary arrests.* There have been many complaints of local residents, unconnected with the dispute, being arrested, usually over an alleged failure to co-operate with the police. Such cases have generally led to eventual release without charge, or to a charge of obstructing the police. However desirable it may be that everyone should co-operate with the police, it is unrealistic to assume that everyone in a deeply divided mining community would welcome the presence or attentions of the police, or wish to assist them beyond the limits of their legal duty. There is no general legal duty to answer police questions or even to co-operate with the police – although some forms of non co-operation will constitute the offence of obstructing the police. In this situation it is particularly important not to be unduly officious, or to demand unquestioning obedience by members of the public. We are sure that senior police officers appreciate this, but we suspect that not all those officers who have been deployed to the mining communities do so. There is a general point here that many officers who have been brought in from elsewhere have not been familiar with their new place of work, either geographically or culturally. We return to this point in our discussion of urban police forces.

(iii) *Rudeness and offensive behaviour.* As on the picket lines, so

15

in the streets of the mining communities, there have been repeated complaints of offensive behaviour by some individual police officers towards striking miners and their families, including insults, highly personal remarks and the waving of pay packets. Such incidents, where they have occurred, must have made the task of the rest of the police even more difficult, not least by creating impressions of partisanship that those who acquire them are apt to attach, however unfairly, to the police as a group.

(iv) *Trespass and assaults on members of the public.* One of the most disturbing aspects of the policing of the dispute is a small number of incidents in which what witnesses described as rampaging groups of police officers have run through mining villages, bursting into houses in pursuit of pickets, causing extensive damage to property and assaulting residents. These incidents require the most thorough and urgent investigation. The action of the Deputy Chief Constable of South Yorkshire in visiting the village of Grimethorpe and publicly apologising to residents for police excesses must have helped to repair some of the damage done to police-community relations. But Grimethorpe has not been the only incident, and apologies and offers of amends have not been evident elsewhere.

(v) *Surveillance.* It is difficult to obtain evidence of what surveillance there has been of striking miners and their representatives. We think it is reasonable to assume that Special Branch police officers have been active in this dispute providing general and specific intelligence to assist police operations. Long before the establishment of the present sophisticated systems for storing and assessing information through the Police National Computer, Special Branch officers were used to pass on useful information about the movement and activities of union leaders and "agitators" from one police force to another, and we assume that this is still done. Such surveillance of individuals engaged in lawful activities in an industrial dispute is not proper, and is a matter which we consider demands public discussion at the earliest possible time. Accordingly, we welcome the recent decision of the Home Affairs Select Committee to investigate the work of the Special Branch, and hope their investigation will extend to these issues.

(vi) *Telephone tapping and interception of correspondence.* One specific area of surveillance on which we have received a number of complaints is the tapping of telephones and interception of mail. The evidence we have so far received does not prove conclusively that such activities have taken place, but in some instances circumstantial evidence in support of the complaints has been very strong. We do not regard the tapping of striking miners' telephones as a justifiable action, or as being within the published statement of the circumstances in which the Home Secretary will authorise the tapping of an individual's telephone. We should welcome any further evidence on this, and call for a clear statement by the Home Secretary on the extent to which telephone tapping has been authorised in connection with the dispute.

The role of officers deployed from the major conurbations

3.25 Many striking miners have commented favourably on the way in which officers of their local police forces have acted during the dispute. Many others have aknowledged a grudging respect for their professionalism, despite anger at the role in which they consider the police have been cast. Favourable comments have also been made about the conduct of members of some of the police forces drafted into the mining areas.

3.26 By contrast, the comments we have received about the Metropolitan Police and officers from some other major cities have frequently been uncomplimentary, and it has been made clear to us privately from police sources that very many police officers from other forces who for the first time have had to work alongside colleagues from these urban forces have not been at all happy with what they have seen.

3.27 Police work away from one's normal area of operations is bound to create difficulties. The style of policing required in large cities is in many respects different from that appropriate to smaller communities anywhere, and mining communities in particular. Police officers who have always lived and worked in a major city may well have more difficulty in appreciating the sense of community, the severity of the impact of unemployment, or the depth of feeling behind the strike in the mining areas, than those who live and work there do. The kind of "macho" police culture recently described in detail by the Policy Studies Institute report on the Metropolitan Police is likely to have reinforced this problem. We believe that the training and briefing of contingents of the Metropolitan and other urban police forces should be reviewed in the light of this. A review is already in hand in the Metropolitan area following the PSI report.

3.28 It is apparent to us that the behaviour of some officers of the Metropolitan Police and of some other forces has seriously tarnished the image of the police as a whole. We must make this point in fairness to the many officers of other forces who have *not* resorted to provocative, heavy-handed, or unruly behaviour.

The impact of the dispute on non-mining areas

3.29 In a number of specific ways the dispute has raised issues of policing which extend beyond the mining areas (although they have arisen within them as well). The issues we have identified under this heading are the effects of the drafting of police to duties connected with the dispute on the standard of "ordinary" policing, particularly within the areas from which they have been drafted; complaints of arrest and harassment of those collecting for miners' support groups and solidarity funds; restrictions on freedom of movement, including road-blocks and restrictions on access to mining areas; and the recording of pickets' vehicle registration numbers on the Police National Computer.

The effect of the dispute on "ordinary" policing

3.30 In some parts of Nottinghamshire, Derbyshire and South Yorkshire, the level of street policing over the past few months has never been so high. No doubt this has served to protect the public from the kinds of crime – such as burglary, theft from parked cars and other street crime – which are likely to be discouraged by very intensive policing. Unfortunately, the rest of England and Wales has seen a significant and sustained depletion of its police resources.

3.31 For a very short period, a police force can accommodate a demand for resources to be sent out of its area by such devices as postponing or cancelling leave, extra overtime, postponing training courses or leaving routine paperwork to be picked up later. Over a period of nine months these expedients are likely to be both insufficient and themselves damaging to the efficiency of the force. We doubt, for a variety of reasons, whether it would be possible to quantify even approximately the effect of the policing of the strike on crime, or to assess its impact on rates of detection or the general quality of the police service. Criminal statistics are at best an unreliable guide to the incidence of crime (some crimes are more likely to be recorded the more efficient the police are at detecting them). Nor is the miners' strike the only factor that will have had a bearing on crime or police work in any particular area (witness the demands on police manpower of increased security against threatened terrorist attacks). However we have no doubt that the standard of service provided by the police in protecting the civil liberties of the public in most areas of the country has been, to a significant degree, adversely affected by the deployment of the police for purposes connected with the strike.

3.32 This conclusion reinforces our view that numbers of police employed on picket duty should not be disproportionate. Every time a thousand police officers are used to escort one man to work, a thousand fewer officers are available to protect the inhabitants of London, Manchester and many other parts of England and Wales from crime, to apprehend criminals, or to respond to accidents or emergencies.

Collections for striking miners and their families

3.33 The strike has brought severe hardship to many of the striking miners and their families. The social security laws exclude strikers from benefit, and benefits for their dependants are subject to an automatic assumption that each striking miner is receiving £15 a week in strike pay, a sum increased from 26th November to £16 a week. We make no comment on the desirability of these provisions, which in their present form were brought into effect by statute in 1980. However they are central to this issue because, over the extended period of this strike and with no strike pay being paid by the NUM, the relief of hardship among the strikers and their families can only be promoted by donations of money and food, and other fund-raising activities.

3.34 We regard the public soliciting of support for a party to an industrial dispute as a legitimate political activity which ought not to be subject to anything other than normal legal controls; in particular the law, and the police, have no business to treat such activities differently according to the nature of the cause, so long as the funds collected are to be used for a lawful purpose. In this respect street collections for striking miners and their families are no different from collections for famine relief or for Christmas presents for needy children.

3.35 The law on street collections is not entirely clear. Generally, it is illegal to collect money on the street without a licence from the local authority, or, in London, the Metropolitan Police Commissioner. (The validity of the regulations applicable to London has been thrown into doubt by a recent decision of a Metropolitan Stipendiary Magistrate). However there is no law against collecting food or selling newspapers.

3.36 We shall return to the question of the law itself in our final report. At this stage we wish to record our concern on two points: first that some local authorities have refused licences for street collections in situations which lead us to suspect that political attitudes towards the purpose of the collection were influential; secondly that other legal provisions have been used against food collectors in situations where they would not have been used against collectors for less contentious causes. On the second point we have received reports of collectors being harassed, threatened with arrest, or arrested, for obstruction of the highway, and in some instances even offences against the Vagrancy Act of 1824. In some cases we have been told that food actually collected was confiscated by the police.

3.37 Obstruction of the highway is notoriously a very broad offence which gives wide discretion to the police. The law is not generally enforced to the letter, and it is vital that the way in which it is enforced should not be thought to depend on a police view of the desirability of the activity being carried on. We have been disturbed by indications of significant disparities in the way the law has been interpreted by those police officers who determine operational policies in different areas. It has also disturbed us that it is evident from much of the information we have received that the law is so unclear in this area that many individual police officers apparently did not know the legal position, when confronted with food collectors, for example.

Road blocks and other restrictions on freedom of movement

3.38 Freedom of movement is a civil liberty we regard as fundamental. It cannot of course be absolute, but we would state as a general principle that anyone should be free to travel on the public highways, wherever he or she wishes, for any lawful purpose. The law allows certain limited restrictions on this freedom, of which the most relevant here is the duty of the police to preserve the peace and prevent crime. The principle of free passage, however, is one that we believe is generally supported. The freedom of working miners to go to work is an important aspect of this freedom, and it is right that the police should protect it (though as we have indicated we do not in all instances endorse the manner and scale of the protection afforded during this dispute). The freedoms of striking miners and members of the public wishing to travel into or through mining areas are equally a part of this freedom, but they have not received the same recognition or protection from the police.

3.39 It is well-known that during this dispute the police have made extensive use of road blocks or road checks. This has been done most frequently in Nottinghamshire and on the boundary between Nottinghamshire and South Yorkshire, but there have also been instances in Derbyshire and other mining areas, and most notably a road block was operated at the Kent entrance to the Dartford tunnel for several days in the early stages of the dispute. The purpose of the police has been variously to dissuade or prevent striking miners from travelling for the purposes of taking part in picketing. Inevitably this has involved stopping other people and questioning them about their identity and destination.

3.40 We have received evidence from many people not connected with the dispute, and from miners travelling for purposes unconnected with the dispute, of police officers at road blocks requiring proof of identity and refusing under threat of arrest to allow people to pass; some non-miners have been arrested for obstructing the police in refusing to comply with instructions to turn back. Miners travelling to picket have reported variously being warned that they would be liable to arrest if they proceeded to a pit to picket, or told to turn back on pain of arrest for obstruction. Some have been arrested in these circumstances. The Chief Constable of Nottinghamshire has stated that altogether 164,508 individuals, whom he described as "presumed pickets", were prevented from entering Nottinghamshire during the first 27 weeks of the strike.

3.41 We are concerned here on three counts. The first is the use of road blocks at all. Police officers have the right in law to require the driver of any motor vehicle to stop, and this power is not limited to regulating the flow of traffic or enforcing road traffic legislation. However, the establishment of road blocks and the stopping of all traffic has no specific legal authorisation. Even under the new Police and Criminal Evidence Act 1984, which received the Royal Assent on 1st November but has not yet come into force, the police will have legal powers to set up "road checks" (either complete or selective road blocks) only in limited circumstances and under specific conditions. In particular a road check will be permissible only to catch the perpetrators of serious offences or escaped prisoners, to locate witnesses, or when authorised by a senior officer who has reasonable ground for suspecting that "a serious arrestable offence is likely to be committed *in that area*" (our italics). It may be that the use of road blocks in areas where violent mass picketing is expected would be authorised by this provision. However the fact that Parliament has thought it necessary to pass a law in these terms (which many MPs considered give the police more power than is desirable) draws attention to the lack of any statutory powers at present. Even when the new law comes into force, road blocks many miles away from the expected picketing will clearly not be justified.

3.42 The second, and more central, concern is the prevention of passage by threatening people with arrest, and actual arrest in some cases where people have insisted on exercising what they believed to be their right of passage past the police check. The police justification for this is their power, indeed duty, to do whatever is necessary to prevent an apprehended breach of the peace. Case law provides that if a police officer has reasonable cause to believe that a breach of the peace will occur in the immediate future and the immediate vicinity unless he or she takes action to prevent it, he or she may take necessary and reasonable preventive action, and in those circumstances it is a criminal obstruction to refuse to comply with his or her directions. The present law does not require the prosecution to prove that the individual charged with obstruction would have committed or caused a breach of the peace if he or she had not been restrained. These legal principles were used by the Attorney-General as a justification for police action in stopping prospective pickets, in a written Parliamentary Answer on 16th March 1984. It is worth quoting in full the central part of this statement, which reads as follows:

"There is no doubt that if a constable reasonably comes to a conclusion that persons are travelling for the purpose of taking part in a picket in circumstances where there is likely to be a breach of the peace, he has the power at common law to call upon them not to continue their journey and to call upon their driver to take them no further. Any person who fails to comply with a police request in those circumstances will be committing the offence of obstructing a police officer in the course of his duty." (Hansard, 16th March 1984, col. 280)

3.43 Just before the completion of this Report the High Court gave its ruling on a test case involving a number of striking miners who were arrested for refusing to turn back at a road block at a motorway exit in Nottinghamshire. Although on the facts the Court ruled that the police were entitled to stop the miners and that their refusal to turn back was a criminal offence, the judgement has laid down important limitations on the powers of the police. Mr Justice Skinner said that there must be reasonable grounds to believe that there was "a real risk of a breach of the peace in the sense that it is in close proximity both in place and time" and that "the imminence and immediacy of the threat to the peace determines what action is reasonable".

3.44 This judgement makes it clear that the police had no power to prevent miners from passing through the Dartford Tunnel, and that the Dartford Tunnnel episode was a serious misuse of police power. The Attorney-General's statement, which was made less than forty-eight hours before the widely criticised Dartford Tunnel incident, can only be interpreted as an attempt to encourage actions which must now been be regarded as legally doubtful.

3.45 We consider the way in which the police have used their powers to stop traffic, in and around Nottinghamshire in particular, goes beyond what is necessary for the preservation of order, and therefore beyond what is justifiable in interfering with individual liberties. In many cases individuals have been inconvenienced or even prevented from making important journeys because the police did not accept their explanations. This smacks of the Soviet internal passport system or South African pass laws. There have moreover been reports of police officers at roadblocks causing gratuitous damage to pickets' cars. The balance between the liberties of working miners to travel to work and of striking miners to picket has been struck almost entirely in favour of the former, creating among the strikers an understandable impression that they were all assumed to be engaged on an enterprise of violence. The attitude to the police of those who did reach the picket lines is unlikely to have been smoothed by these experiences, and the primary task of the police, of keeping order on the spot, may well have been made more difficult as a result.

3.46 We also regard the way in which road blocks and road checks have been used, most particularly away from the immediate areas where picketing has taken place, as operationally unwise. We do not wish to imply by this that the police should have abstained from affording protection to working miners, or securing the preservation of order, nor that we regard violence or intimidation by mass pickets as acceptable. We have made our views on these points clear already. Reliance on a policy of passive containment of pickets would, in our view, have generally been wiser, and would at the same time have avoided a very clear impression being created that the police regard picketing, or at least secondary picketing, as criminal in itself and certain to lead to violence. In the light of the High Court case, policy on road blocks should be reviewed by the police and their advisers.

3.47 The third point of concern is the intensity of the police operation, particularly in Nottinghamshire, and the degree of intrusion into the lives of local residents this has entailed. We have already referred to some aspects of this, and here we are concerned with restrictions on freedom to travel. Many residents of Nottinghamshire and adjacent areas, who need to travel regularly for reasons, business or otherwise, unconnected with the dispute have been stopped and questioned about their identity and destination so frequently as to amount to harassment. Some may regard this as a small price to pay for the preservation of order, and be grateful to the police for their diligence. But the freedom to travel without official interference is a freedom not lightly to be discarded; police checks every few miles or on occasions more frequently have only been seen exceptionally in this country, in the course of major murder hunts or searches for dangerous escaped prisoners. They should not be allowed to become in any way an expected police response to serious disorder, let alone be allowed to drift into becoming part of "normal policing".

Recording of pickets' car registration numbers

3.48 Mr Douglas Hurd, then a Home Office Minister, stated in a Parliamentary Answer on 20th June 1984 that the police were recording the registration numbers of vehicles used by pickets on the Police National Computer. Numbers were (and, so far as we know, still are) being placed in the stolen and suspect vehicles index under the category of vehicles seen or checked in noteworthy circumstances. This category is "weeded" if there is no further sighting within 14 days. In the meantime the obvious consequence of the information being stored is that if the same vehicle is stopped again at a road check the police officer who radios in the registration number will get a positive response to his inquiry.

3.49 We regard this practice as unacceptable for two reasons. The first is that it subjects people to surveillance (which might not have come to light but for a Parliamentary Question) and an invasion of their personal privacy purely as a result of their participation in picketing. No offence need be involved, and again the implicit assumptions as to the nature of *all* picketing are clear. The second is that it is likely to undermine public confidence in the way in which the police record and store information by computer. We accept that the use of computers to store criminal records and to assist in the prevention of crime is a desirable development but only if it is subject to proper safeguards. The public tends to be suspicious of computer records, and any evidence that they have been used for improper purposes will lead to an undermining of public trust in the principle of computerised police records.

The administration of criminal justice

3.50 Because the legal system in Scotland is different from that in England and Wales, there have been important differences in procedure in relation to the dispute. Some of our concerns are specific to England and Wales, and in the points under this heading our comments relate only to England and Wales unless the contrary is stated. We intend in our Final Report to highlight any special points relevant to Scotland.

Arrest and the treatment of those arrested

3.51 From the start of the miners' strike until 8th November, 7,658 arrests were made in England and Wales alone in connection with the dispute. Another 1,228 people were arrested and charged in Scotland up to 26th October. By the time our Report is published these figures will be substantially larger. What is most worrying about this is that such a large number of people, the great majority of whom have had no previous dealings with the police or the criminal courts, should have been brought into the criminal law enforcement system as a result of the dispute. Our immediate concerns, however, are more specific.

3.52 The first concern is the number of people who have been arrested but, subsequently charged with any offence. Of the 7,658 people arrested in England and Wales up to 8th November, no less than 1,302, or 17%, were not charged. (The figures for Scotland do not differentiate between arrests and charges.) To some extent this may reflect a commendably rigorous approach by charge officers (who must be satisfied that there is sufficient evidence before accepting a charge). However we are concerned that it also indicates that arrest has on occasion been used to remove people from the scene of trouble for a period rather than for its proper purpose of taking them into custody as a first step in the prosecution of an alleged offence. We suspect in particular that this has occurred where people have been arrested for refusal to answer questions to the satisfaction of police officers at road blocks, or in connection with street food collections. We should welcome more evidence on this point.

3.53 We have also been concerned by evidence we have received on a number of points in connection with the treatment of those arrested. At its most serious, this has included allegations of serious assaults on those in custody. We are not in a position to comment on individual allegations, save to say that any allegation of assault in police custody must be very carefully investigated.

3.54 We have also seen allegations that miners and their wives, while in custody after arrest, were questioned by the police about their political beliefs, including such matters as their views about Mr Scargill and how they voted at the last General Election. Such questioning by the police, if it has occurred as alleged, is a grossly improper misuse of authority, and likely to create suspicions of partisanship by the police that can only further damage police-community relationships. We should welcome more evidence on this and the previous point.

3.55 Complaints have been made about the physical conditions under which those arrested were subsequently detained. Conditions were not necessarily any worse for those arrested in connection with the dispute than for other arrested persons, save to the extent that large numbers of prisoners overload the system. The effect of large scale arrests however has been to produce, on occasions, gross overcrowding of cells for extended periods and we have been told of instances of police vans being used for the temporary detention of arrested persons because the police station was too full. These specific points apart, we feel that the bringing into police custody of large numbers of normally law abiding individuals who had never seen the inside of a police cell before has served to highlight some of the more general inadequacies of conditions of police custody. We do not suggest that miners, or indeed MPs, should be treated any differently in custody from others, but we do suggest that the quality of the accommodation and the procedures for dealing with individual prisoners both need to be reviewed. We hope that the appointment of lay visitors, currently the subject of an experiment in South Yorkshire, will lead to these matters receiving more scrutiny. However we are surprised that, according to the Chairman of the South Yorkshire Police Authority, no miners have been visited in custody during the South Yorkshire experiment.

3.56 Two specific aspects of conditions of detention that concern us are access to a solicitor and notification of arrest to a relative. We have been told of several instances where both were long delayed or withheld; anxious relatives have been given no indication of the fact that a husband, wife, parent or child was in police custody, and solicitors were denied access to their clients. There is a statutory right to have notification of arrest sent to a relative or friend, and, while at present the right to see a solicitor is provided for only in the non-statutory Judges' Rules, it too will become a statutory right on the coming into force of the Police and Criminal Evidence Act. Although both rights are subject to exceptions, these are specific and limited, and do not confer a general discretion on the police to withhold them to suit operational convenience. Our view on the evidence we have so far received is that on occasions the latter criterion may have been used.

3.57 The police may understimate the importance of giving effect to these rights, and the influx of a large number of arrested persons into a normally quiet police station undoubtedly creates problems. However these are not sufficient excuses to deny legal rights, especially when, as has been the case with most of those arrested in connection with the strike, they are later charged with only relatively minor offences for which immediate police bail would, in other circumstances, have been granted, or are released subsequently without being charged at all.

3.58 Evidence has also been given to us of reluctance by the police, particularly in Nottinghamshire, to release people on bail once they have been charged. In particular it has been suggested to us by solicitors and others that people have been remanded in custody until the next sitting of the magistrates' court for offences which in the past, or if unconnected with the dispute, would have been considered suitable for police bail. Such practices amount to the use of custody as a form of punishment meted out by the police on the basis of their assessment of the case, a procedure wholly alien to British traditions of justice. We consider that those responsible for policy on police bail should take immediate steps to ensure that, if bail is being withheld in cases where it would have been granted had the offences alleged not been connected with the strike, the practice is discontinued at once.

Choice of charges

3.59 Those arrested up to 8th November in England and Wales have been charged with a total of 8,194 offences, ranging from riot and arson to trespassing on the railway line. We wish to stress that the majority of the charges are of relatively minor offences. The four most numerous allegations, accounting for 77% of all charges, are conduct likely to lead to a breach of the peace, obstructing the police, criminal damage and obstructing the highway. In Scotland the majority of charges have also been of minor offences, usually breach of the peace or obstructing the police. However we wish to draw attention to two aspects of the range of charges that appear to us to be a source of concern.

3.60 The first is the large number of individuals charged with riotous or unlawful assembly (137 and 502 cases respectively, together representing almost 8% of all charges). These are broad common law offences which carry a possible penalty of life imprisonment (a point to which the Home Secretary has drawn pointed, and, in our view, injudicious, public attention). The scope of these offences is rather vague, and was criticised in a recent report by the Law Commission, which recommended that they should be replaced by rather narrower statutory crimes. In Scotland there have been no charges, so far as we are aware, of the equivalent crime of mobbing or rioting. Although the police may prosecute without the consent of the Director of Public Prosecutions, we think it extremely unlikely that the use of these charges on a scale unprecedented in recent years can have followed from a decision of the police alone.

3.61 The use of old, broad and potentially draconian laws in this way is a worrying development. These cases must also be tried by jury, and we anticipate that it will be impossible to find juries completely uninfluenced by what they have seen and read about the dispute. Moreover the delay involved in cases coming to trial will mean that the last cases are likely to drag on well into 1985 or even 1986.

3.62 The second point is the revival of the hitherto almost unused, and somewhat arcane, offence of "watching and besetting" under section 7 of the Conspiracy, and Protection of Property Act 1875. Given the range of other charges available to the police in situations to which this colourfully named offence might be appropriate, and given that there is no power to arrest for it, we find the presence of 226 charges worrying. The use of a charge that has been almost unknown in recent industrial relations history can also appear as an attempt to "throw the book" at those arrested, with the likely result of further damaging the perception of the police by striking miners and their families and supporters.

Bail conditions

3.63 Most of those charged with criminal offences have been released on bail by the courts. However in a very large proportion of those cases the bail has been subject to conditions. In Mansfield Magistrates' Court in particular (where those arrested in Notting-hamshire have generally been taken for their first court appear-ance) it has been standard practice to grant bail subject to a condition "not to visit any premises or place for the purpose of picketing or demonstrating in connection with the current trade dispute between the National Union of Mineworkers and the National Coal Board other than peacefully to picket or demons-trate at your usual place of employment". This condition, on a pre-printed slip of paper, is stapled to the form recording the decision to grant bail.

3.64 In some cases variations to these "usual conditions" have been made, including restrictions on residence (in one extreme Nottinghamshire case, according to newspaper reports, a require-ment to reside with a relative in Caithness) and prohibitions on leaving home at certain times of day. However the typical pattern on days when large numbers of people have been brought before the court has been for the "usual conditions" to be applied so routinely to every case that the Lord Chief Justice felt it necessary to suggest that the Clerk to the Court should not affix the slip of paper to the bail form until after the defendant's application for unconditional bail had been heard and considered.

3.65 The legality of the "usual conditions" has been challenged in the High Court, which on October 12th ruled that they were not in breach of the Bail Act 1976. The Lord Chief Justice also ruled that Magistrates were entitled to use their knowledge of events at local collieries during the preceding weeks. We understand that that ruling was based in part on unchallenged police evidence about the violent nature of the picketing. However the point has been decided and we must accept that the conditions are lawful. That does not mean that they are necessarily desirable. We consider that they are undesirable, contrary to the spirit of the Bail Act and a serious incursion on some of the fundamental liberties we identify in Section 2 of this Report.

3.66 One fundamental liberty to which we have referred in Section 2 is the presumption of innocence in criminal trials. People who apply for bail pending their trial have not yet been convicted, and are entitled to the presumption of innocence. In practical terms this cannot be absolute – we do not imagine, for instance, that society would tolerate the granting of bail to those charged with multiple murders. However it is embodied in the spirit of the Bail Act, which requires that bail should be granted unless a remand in custody is necessary for a specific reason, and that conditions should not be imposed on bail unless they too are necessary. One permissible ground for withholding bail or imposing conditions is the likelihood of the defendant committing a "further" offence (we use quotation marks to highlight the inconsistency between this concept and the presumption that the defendant is innocent of any offence until proved guilty). In this context we would expect that the absence of a previous criminal record would be a relevant consideration, as would the nature of the offence alleged, and not merely the fact that it was connected in some way with the coal dispute.

3.67 The effect of the bail conditions is to prevent altogether secondary picketing. The fact that the "usual conditions" differentiate between picketing at the defendant's place of work and picketing elsewhere can only be explained adequately on that basis. But secondary picketing is a *civil* wrong, not a criminal offence, and there is no provision in the Bail Act which allows the courts to use bail to prevent a breach of the civil law, any more than it is the duty of the police to do so. It is an unfortunate consequence of the Lord Chief Justice's judgement that bail conditions can now be used as a substitute for civil law remedies in this way.

3.68 Freedom of movement, and freedom to demonstrate, including participation in peaceful picketing, are important and basic freedoms which should not be curtailed even temporarily, except under clear justification. We do not accept that there is an automatic justification for curtailing the freedom of an individual to take part in demonstrations in support of the striking miners merely because he or she is alleged to have committed an offence in connection with the same dispute. There is a dangerous principle implicit in the assumption that those who commit offences in connection with industrial disputes are more likely to commit further offences than "ordinary" offenders, which could well be applied equally to political demonstrators, with even clearer restrictions on freedom resulting.

3.69 The consequences of conditional bail of this kind can be, and on the evidence we have received appear on occasion to have been in this dispute, more drastic than the likely consequences of conviction for the original offence. Most of those so far dealt with by the courts for offences in connection with the dispute have been fined. Bail conditions in similar cases involve more drastic curtailments of liberty than the subsequent fines. In particular they expose those on conditional bail to the risk of harassment by the police while going about their lawful business, and to immediate incarceration, through revocation of bail, on being caught at the scene of a perfectly lawful demonstration. In one well publicised case, Mr Malcolm Pitt, President of the Kent Area NUM, was imprisoned for 19 days for breach of a condition of bail not to take part in picketing or demonstrations other than at his usual place of work, but was subsequently only fined for the offence which had given rise to the bail conditions.

3.70 Our final and most significant concern is that the way in which bail conditions have been routinely and uniformly applied to widely differing cases creates an impression of what one defendant aptly described as "supermarket justice". Nothing would more rapidly bring the British system of criminal justice into disrepute than for the impression to be given that cases were dealt with according to predetermined rules without consideration of the individual merits of each case. That impression has in our view been created by the way in which magistrates' courts, and in particular that at Mansfield, have handled the question of bail.

Trial procedure

3.71 We hope in our final report to be able to comment in more detail on the way in which cases arising from the dispute have been dealt with in the courts. So far only a relatively small proportion of cases have been concluded, and the backlog of cases has led the Lord Chancellor to appoint additional stipendiary magistrates for Nottinghamshire to catch up with some of the work.

3.72 The results of a research project currently under way into the disposition of cases connected with the dispute in magistrates' courts will be available to us for our final report, and we shall look in particular at whether there are discrepancies between the way in which local lay magistrates, with knowledge of the localities and their problems, deal with cases and the ways in which they are dealt with by stipendiary magistrates. One preliminary indication we have from figures available is that the proportion of defendants in cases connected with the dispute who are acquitted is markedly higher than the proportion of acquittals in all cases before magistrates' courts and we shall be particularly interested to examine evidence of why this should be so – whether, for instance, it reflects a higher proportion of the cases being contested.

3.73 Another aspect of trial procedure which we intend to examine in our final report is the pattern of granting and refusing legal aid to defendants. Legal aid in Magistrates' Courts and the Sheriff Court is a matter of discretion, and previous research has shown that the exercise of this discretion varies widely between courts. It has been suggested to us that some courts, especially in some areas of Scotland, have been less favourably disposed to grant legal aid in cases connected with the dispute, but without more detailed research we are not in a position to comment on this. However it is extremely rare for legal aid to be refused for cases that are to be tried by jury, and we should be very concerned at any significant pattern of refusals in cases where the offences alleged are sufficiently serious to entail jury trial.

Binding over

3.74 We are concerned at the way in which binding over orders have been used during the current dispute. The binding over order is not technically a conviction (although there is a right of appeal against it) but it clearly carries a significant stigma, and ought not in our view to be imposed except on specific grounds duly established before a court. We have been informed of cases where defendants appearing before the courts charged with criminal offences were effectively offered an alternative of accepting a binding over order or being tried for the substantive offences. This puts those who wish to dispute their guilt – and who may indeed not be guilty – into an intolerable position, where they must either risk conviction and sentence, and incidentally a further period on remand, probably on conditional bail, or agree to be bound over to keep the peace, on pain of forfeiture of a possibly substantial sum of money.

3.75 We can see no justification for the use of binding over orders in this way, other than to reduce the backlog on the courts. We regard it as the responsibility of the proper authorities to ensure that sufficient magistrates and courts are made available to hear cases properly, rather than to use shortcuts to reduce the backlog of cases without sufficient regard to the position of individual defendants, and we call on those concerned to use binding over orders only on proof of a criminal offence for which a binding over order would be appropriate.

The organisation and accountability of the police

3.76 Some of the issues under this heading raise longer term implications to which we shall wish to return in more detail in our Final Report, and in this Interim Report we deal only briefly with them. This is not intended to indicate that they are less important. In the longer term we believe that the questions about the accountability of the police raised by the policing of the strike are among the most fundamental questions to which a solution will have to be sought if civil liberties are to be properly safeguarded.

The National Reporting Centre, the Home Secretary and the Association of Chief Police Officers

3.77 The existence of the National Reporting Centre (NRC) at Scotland Yard was little known before the miners' strike, and its functions in the past have been limited. There have been statutory arrangements for nearly 100 years for Chief Constables to provide "mutual aid" to reinforce the strength of another force. Typically this provision has been used to provide extra manpower to deal with a short-term policing problem such as a major demonstration or a local football Derby. Consequently the full implications of mutual aid have not been widely discussed, or perhaps even fully considered by those concerned.

3.78 During this dispute the scale of mutual aid has been massive and its duration protracted. It has fallen to the NRC not merely to monitor but in effect to manage the redeployment of large bodies of police officers in England and Wales on a weekly basis. The organisation of mutual aid through the NRC has been the responsibility of whichever Chief Constable has for the time being been President of the Association of Chief Police Officers (ACPO).

3.79 Some procedure may be necessary for the co-ordination of policing on such a major scale, if only in the interest of efficiency.

This does not necessarily mean that the establishment of the NRC, which was never expressly approved by Parliament, is acceptable either in concept or operation. The way that it operates has given rise to a number of questions and expressions of concern to which we shall return in more detail in our final report. These include the question of who is accountable to whom for the NRC; the relationship between the NRC and individual Chief Constables and the extent to which Chief Constables have retained any freedom to balance the policing needs of their own areas against the requests for mutual aid; the relationship of the NRC to the Home Secretary and the extent to which the police service as a whole has been subjected to Governmental decisions on questions of operational policy; and the working of the usual chains of command in those areas where police from other parts of the country have been temporarily imported.

3.80 On the last point, a central principle of mutual aid is that police officers working in the area of another force are subject to the instructions of senior officers of that force as if they were on full secondment. It has been suggested to us that this has not always happened in practice, and that what has happened has come close to the setting up of a national police riot squad, independent of local police management and accountable to a central organisation. We are not yet in a position to comment fully on these points, but we feel bound at this stage to acknowledge the issues. We should welcome more evidence on matters relevant to these central questions, and on the very closely related question of accountability, to which we now turn.

Accountability to local police authorities

3.81 Outside London, the local police authority for each force has statutory responsibilities for ensuring the provision of an efficient police force (the precise scope of these responsibilities differs between England and Wales and Scotland). Half of the costs of the police service are required to be met from local authority funds. It has long been a matter of debate how far these responsibilities confer rights on police authorities to scrutinise and be consulted on the policies of their chief constable. It is generally accepted that the role of police authorities stops short of involvement in operational decisions, but the boundary between operational and policy matters has never been adequately defined. However the existence of a degree of local accountability is in our view an essential element of an efficient and publicly acceptable police force, able to police by the consent of at least the majority of the community it serves. Lord Scarman recognised the importance of this in his report on the Brixton Disorders of 1981 (Cmnd. 8427) in which he recommended the introduction of a statutory requirement on the police to consult representatives of the community; this proposal, which we consider to be no more than a first step in the direction of effective accountability, was subsequently accepted by the Government and has been implemented in the Police and Criminal Evidence Act 1984.

3.82 Relationships between a number of police authorities and their Chief Constables had deteriorated as a result of disputes over accountability before the miners' strike. However, the impact of the policing of the strike has caused further rifts, leading in the case of South Yorkshire to litigation, in Merseyside to the censuring of the Chief Constable, and in Greater Manchester to a formal request by the Chief Constable to the Home Secretary for a definition of his responsibilities. The question raised by the Chief Constable of Greater Manchester demands an answer, but not only on the basis of what the law is now. The immediate questions are: to whom is the Chief Constable responsible and for what, and who will answer for him when members of the public wish to call him to account? There is also the wider question: to whom *should* he be responsible and for what?

3.83 The difficulties of the police authorities' position have been magnified by the operation of mutual aid. So far as we can tell, police authorities have been given no say in whether, or how many, police officers should be sent from their area to police the picket lines. Their responsibility to maintain an efficient police force in their area cannot be maintained if too many officers are removed from their service. The matter is complicated by the financial arrangements: because the mutual aid has been classified by the Home Office as "large scale" rather than "major", salaries are still payable by the sending authority, with the recipient authority responsible only for travelling and other additional costs of the deployment. Arrangements for the reimbursement of additional costs have not proved entirely satisfactory at a time when local authority spending is so closely controlled.

3.84 In these circumstances, it is quite understandable that many police authorities feel the existing system of political and financial responsibility has collapsed. For our Final Report we hope to have available the results of a detailed survey of the police authorities' responses to the strike, and we should welcome any other evidence, especially from members of police authorities and Chief Constables, about how local accountability has operated in practice and how for the future a system of proper local accountability, which we believe to be an essential prerequisite of good policing, can be secured.

Accountability and complaints procedures

3.85 An important aspect of any system of accountability is the manner in which complaints by individual members of the public are dealt with. In our Introduction we have pointed to the lack of any formal machinery to deal with complaints about operational decisions, in contrast to the arrangements for complaints about the actions of individual police officers. The system for investigating the latter kind of complaint is governed by the Police Acts of 1964 and 1976 in England and Wales, and in Scotland by the Police (Scotland) Act 1967. Lord Scarman found that a "lack of confidence" in the system was revealed in the evidence submitted to the Inquiry into the Brixton Disorders. The Police and Criminal Evidence Act 1984 will introduce a new procedure for dealing with complaints in England and Wales, under the supervision of a new Police Complaints Authority. It would be premature for us to comment in detail on how far this will meet criticisms of the existing system, save to say that the failure to introduce comparable elements of independence into the Scottish system will inevitably leave that system open to serious criticism. We do however wish to express our concern about one matter which affects equally the present and the new complaints procedures in England and Wales, and the procedure in Scotland.

3.86 In order for a complaint about an individual police officer to be pursued, it must be possible for the officer to be identified. Normally all police officers in uniform wear an identifying numeral which is not only a symbol of their personal accountability but a reasonably effective means of identifying a particular officer against whom an allegation is made. We have received several reports of police officers on picket duty wearing protective clothing which concealed their numerals. The complaints system is easily brought into disrepute if those against whom members of the public wish to lodge complaints cannot be identified – in the circumstances of this strike even the force to which they belong may not be readily ascertainable. We make no complaint about police officers being issued with necessary protective clothing, but it must carry appropriate individual identification.

CONCLUSION

We have issued this Interim Report because of our concern for the state of civil liberty during the miners' strike, and the longer term effects the strike may have on liberty. We have set out to view the issues raised by the strike from the standpoint of civil liberties. We believe that this standpoint has not been sufficiently respected or appreciated in either the conduct or the public discussion of this strike. Our hope in publishing this Report is that the erosion of civil liberties will be more widely noticed and discussed, and that there will be a serious effort on the part of all concerned not to allow the competing goals of the protagonists to be the occasion for any futher erosion of basic freedom, now or after the strike.

In this spirit we conclude with four immediate pleas:

–That all those involved in the strike and the police operations should, so long as the strike continues, refrain from violence, intimidation or any other actions likely to cause injury or public disorder or provoke unnecessary ill-feeling in any way;

–That the strike should not be used as an excuse for precipitate legislation restricting civil liberties;

–That the erosion of the liberties of the public during this strike should not be left as a permanent memorial to the conflict;

–That the Government should agree to the establishment of formal parliamentary or judicial inquiry into the range of issues discussed in this report.

PETER WALLINGTON (CHAIRMAN)
JOHN ALDERSON
LARRY GOSTIN
SARAH McCABE
IAN MARTIN
CHRISTOPHER MASON
26th November 1984